HORSE — 30 MILES (48 KM) PER HOUR

SKATEBOARD — 15 MILES (24 KM) PER HOUR

DOG — 20 MILES (32 KM) PER HOUR

STOCK CAR — 190 MILES (306 KM) PER HOUR   NOW THAT'S FAST!: STOCK CARS

JACKRABBIT — 45 MILES (72 KM) PER HOUR

HUMAN — 12 MILES (19 KM) PER HOUR

BICYCLE — 15 MILES (24 KM) PER HOUR

NOW THAT'S FAST!

STOCK CARS

KATE RIGGS

CREATIVE EDUCATION

Published by Creative Education
P.O. Box 227, Mankato, Minnesota 56002
Creative Education is an imprint of
The Creative Company
www.thecreativecompany.us

Book and cover design by Blue Design
(www.bluedes.com)
Art direction by Rita Marshall
Printed in the United States of America

Photographs by Dreamstime (Actionsports,
Walleyelj), Getty Images (John Harrelson/
NASCAR, Robert Laberge/NASCAR, Nick
Laham, RacingOne, Jamie Squire, Matthew
Stockman, Todd Warshaw/NASCAR, Frank
Whitney), iStockphoto (Michael Krinke)

Library of Congress Cataloging-in-
Publication Data
Riggs, Kate.
Stock cars / by Kate Riggs.
p. cm. — (Now that's fast!)
Includes index.
Summary: A quick-paced, colorful
description of the physical characteristics,
purposes, early history, and high-speed
capabilities of NASCAR stock cars—the
fastest cars in stock car racing.
ISBN 978-1-58341-916-8
1. Stock cars (Automobiles)—Juvenile
literature. 2. Automobile racing—Juvenile
literature. I. Title. II. Series.

TL236.28.R54 2010
629.228—dc22
2009002757

First Edition
9 8 7 6 5 4 3 2 1

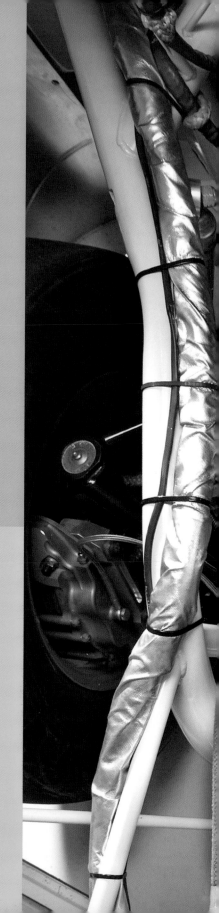

A stock car is a kind of race car. Stock cars have special **engines** that help them go fast. Most stock cars can go almost 200 miles (322 km) per hour!

A stock car engine has a lot of tubes and metal parts in it

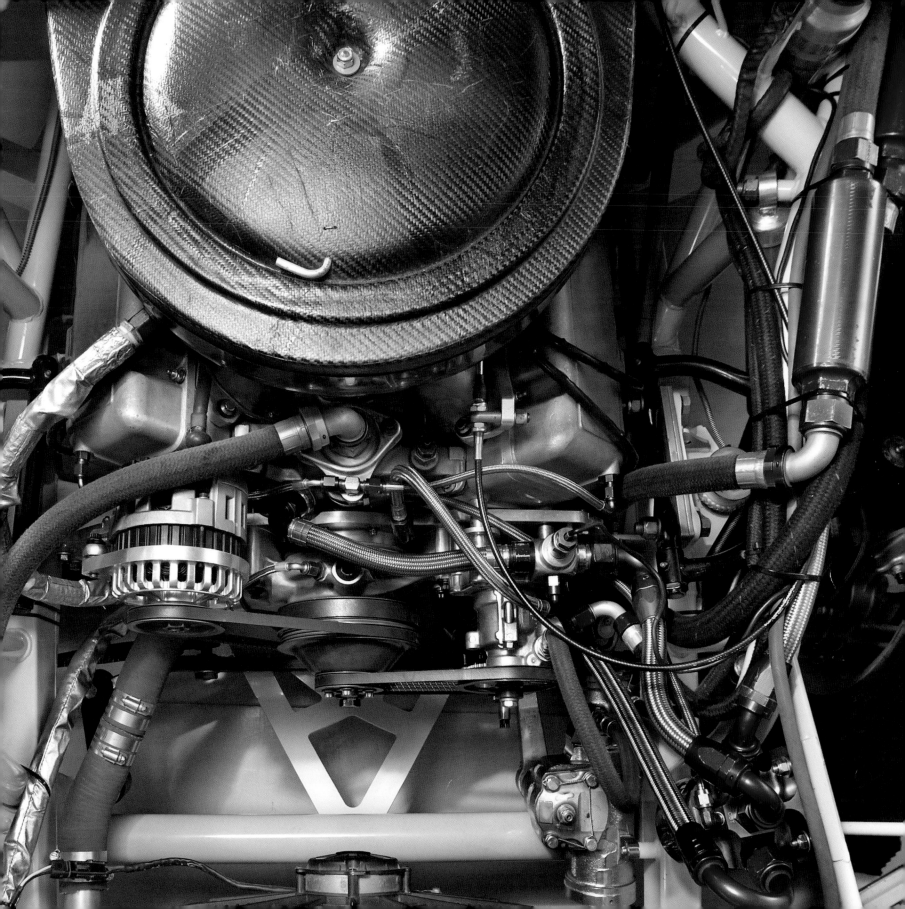

Stock cars are used for racing. They race around an O-shaped track. The track is not very long. But the cars race for 200 to 600 miles (322–966 km). One race can take more than three hours to finish.

STOCK CARS

Stock cars look like normal cars. But they can go a lot faster. Each car has a **roll cage**. This frame helps keep the driver safe if the car crashes.

There is not much space for the driver to sit inside a stock car

The driver uses the steering wheel to control the car. Stock cars weigh less than normal cars do. This helps them go faster. It is easy to tell each car apart. A stock car has the names of its **sponsors** on the outside.

Pennzoil is an oil company that sponsors stock cars in races

The first stock cars were made in the 1930s. People built stock cars from normal car parts. Then the National Association for Stock Car Auto Racing (NASCAR) was formed in 1948. Soon, stock cars started racing each other all across the United States.

In the 1940s, cars raced on the sand at Daytona Beach in Florida

All stock cars have the same basic **design**. NASCAR wants all stock cars to be made the same way. That way, all the racers have the same chance of winning.

STOCK CARS

Stock cars that race on **superspeedways** have a part added to their engines. A piece of metal called a restrictor plate keeps the cars from going more than 190 miles (306 km) per hour.

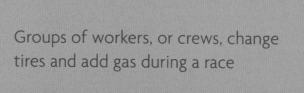

Groups of workers, or crews, change tires and add gas during a race

When stock cars race on superspeedways, they zoom around the curves. Sometimes they bunch together. They go around and around the track for a long time!

The Talladega Superspeedway is in the state of Alabama

Stock car drivers make their cars
go very fast. They steer away from
other cars so they do not crash.
Every driver hopes to win the race!

Fast Facts

Jimmie Johnson and Jeff Gordon are two famous stock car drivers from the U.S.

Cars can go as fast as 208 miles (335 km) per hour in some NASCAR races.

The Sprint Cup is the most important racing series for stock cars in the U.S.

Stock car racing is popular outside the U.S. in countries such as Great Britain and Canada.

Glossary

design—a plan that shows how something will look and how it will work

engines—machines inside vehicles that make them move

roll cage—a frame of metal bars that is built into the sides and top of a stock car

series—a set of events

sponsors—companies that support a racing team with money

superspeedways—the longest racetracks; they are usually about 2.5 miles (4 km) long

Read More about It

Bullard, Lisa. *Stock Cars*. Minneapolis: Lerner Publications, 2004.

Gutelle, Andrew. *Stock Car Kings*. New York: Grosset & Dunlap, 2001.

Web Site

KidzWorld NASCAR trivia
http://www.kidzworld.com/quiz/4479-quiz-nascar-trivia
This site has a fun quiz about NASCAR.

Index